The Essential Bone Broth Cookbook

Simple Recipes for D

Stocks and Bases

BY: SOPHIA FREEMAN

© 2019 Sophia Freeman All Rights Reserved

* * * ★ * ★ ★ ★ * ★ * * * *

COPYRIGHTED

Liability

This publication is meant as an informational tool. The individual purchaser accepts all liability if damages occur because of following the directions or guidelines set out in this publication. The Author bears no responsibility for reparations caused by the misuse or misinterpretation of the content.

Copyright

The content of this publication is solely for entertainment purposes and is meant to be purchased by one individual. Permission is not given to any individual who copies, sells or distributes parts or the whole of this publication unless it is explicitly given by the Author in writing.

Table of Contents

Introduction

Are you looking for new and delicious broths and stocks to use for soups, sauces and gravy? Do you want more bone broth recipes for tastier foods with less waste? Then look no further than this essential cookbook for all of your broth needs. From beef to vegetable, making the perfect stock for your soup or gravy is simple and satisfying. The taste of fresh stock is better than any store-bought package.

1. Pressure cooker beef stock

During the holidays, I like to make my beef gravy for dinner with some fresh biscuits and mashed potatoes. This gravy adds taste to the plate, including green beans.

Preparation Time-10 minutes

Servings-14

Ingredients

- 16 ounces beef bones
- 1 large unpeeled sweet onion, halved
- 4 large carrots, sliced into 4" medallions
- 4 ribs celery, sliced into 4" pieces
- 1 bunch flat-leaf parsley
- 4 halved garlic cloves
- ½ ounce salt
- 1 teaspoon dried thyme
- 1 teaspoon whole black peppercorns
- 2 bay leaves
- 192 ounces water

Directions

1. Preheat oven to 425 degrees Fahrenheit

2. Arrange bones on a baking sheet and bake for 15-20 minutes.

3. Arrange onions on the baking sheet and bake for another 45 minutes.

4. Transfer beef bones and onion to a pressure cooker and add the rest of the Ingredients.

5. Cover the cooker with the lid and set according to Directions for 1 hour.

6. Remove cooker from heat and open lid carefully

2. Homemade chicken stock

After a winter of colds and flus, I tried this chicken stock to make a healthy chicken soup. The flavour and warmth of the broth cured whatever ailed me.

Preparation Time-10 minutes

Servings-12

Ingredients

- 48 ounces chicken backs and necks
- 1 unpeeled large onion, sliced into 6 pieces
- 2 chunked carrots
- 1 chunked celery stalk
- 2 peeled garlic cloves
- 4 sprigs fresh thyme, chopped
- 1 bay leaf
- 96 ounces cold water

Directions

1. Mix all Ingredients in a large pot and bring to a simmer on medium low heat. Skim fat off the surface of the stock as it simmers.

2. Simmer for 12 hours, skimming as you go.

3. Remove pot from heat and cool for 2 hours. Pour the broth through a fine mesh strainer into a large sealable container.

3.Slow cooker vegan stock

Meat bones are the not the only foods you can turn into broth. This vegan stock adds delicious flavour to soups and sauces without the meat.

Preparation Time-25 minutes

Servings-8

Ingredients

- 1 ounce extra-virgin olive oil
- 4 stalks celery, sliced into 4" pieces
- 2 chopped carrots
- 1 chopped potato
- 1 onion, sliced into 8 wedges
- 2 large outer romaine lettuce leaves
- 4 ounces gluten-free beer
- 2 shallots, cut in half
- Outer layers only of 1 fennel bulb
- 1/8 apple
- ½ green pepper
- 9 whole black peppercorns
- ¼ bunch flat-leaf parsley
- 1 lemon wedge
- 1" piece ginger
- 1 ounce tamari
- ½ ounce vegan Worcestershire sauce
- 1 bay leaf
- 2 cloves garlic
- 64 ounces cold water

Directions

1. Grease the bottom of a slow cooker with olive oil. Add all Ingredients to the slow cooker and cook for 4 hours on High or Low for 8-10 hours.

2. Strain Ingredients in the slow cooker into a large bowl.

3. Place cheesecloth in a strainer and pour the Ingredients through the strainer and into a sealable container

4.Slow cooker bone broth

I like to use apple cider vinegar that is organic and has the "mother". This type of vinegar is healthier and it is filmier than the processed stuff.

Preparation Time-25 minutes

Servings-8

Ingredients

- 48 ounces beef bones
- 3 chopped carrots
- 2 chopped celery stalks
- 1 chopped onion
- 5 smashed garlic cloves,
- 2 bay leaves
- 1 teaspoon whole black peppercorns
- cold water
- 1 ounce apple cider vinegar
- kosher salt

Directions

1. Preheat oven to 375 degrees Fahrenheit

2. Line a baking sheet with foil and arrange beef bones on the sheet in one layer.

3. Place baking sheet in the oven and cook for 25-30 minutes

4. Place celery, carrots, peppercorns, onion, garlic and bay leaves in a slow cooker. Top with bones and pour in water to cover the bones.

5. Pour in apple cider vinegar and sprinkle with salt.

6. Cook on Low for 8-10 hours or High for 4 hours. Strain the broth through a fine mesh sieve and discard large pieces of food.

5.Bone Broth

This recipe is perfect for leftover beef shanks and makes a delicious base for beef stew. You can freeze this broth for up to 6 months if sealed properly.

Preparation Time-10 minutes

Servings-8

Ingredients

- cooking spray
- 6 ounces tomato paste
- 32 ounces beef bones
- 48 ounces cold water
- 2 thickly sliced onions
- 2 chopped carrots
- 3 crushed cloves garlic
- 2 bay leaves

Directions

1. Preheat oven to 400 degrees Fahrenheit. Coat a roasting pan with cooking spray.

2. Spread paste on beef bones and arrange in roasting pan.

3. Bake for 30 minutes until beef bones start to brown

4. Add the rest of the ingredients to a slow cooker and cook for 24 hours on Low.

5. Strain mixture through a fine mesh sieve into a sealable container and chill in the refrigerator until ready to use.

6. Weekend Chicken Stock

I like to make this chicken stock on the weekend so I can take my time with it. The longer it cooks, the more the flavours blend.

Preparation Time-20 minutes

Servings-16

Ingredients

- ½ ounce extra-virgin olive oil
- carcasses of 2 rotisserie chicken, chopped into pieces
- 4 chopped carrots
- 2 large chopped onions
- 3 chopped stalks celery
- 4 ounces dry white wine
- 5 whole cloves
- ½ ounce whole peppercorns
- 1 sprig fresh thyme
- 2 bay leaves
- 160 ounces water

Directions

1. Preheat oven to 400 degrees Fahrenheit

2. Grease a large roasting pan with olive oil. Add carcass pieces, onions, carrots and celery

3. Roast for 1 hour, stirring occasionally until mixture is browned

4. Transfer mixture from roasting pan to a large pot.

5. Pour white wine in the roasting pan and scrape the pan clean of food particles. Pour wine and particles into the slow cooker.

6. Add the rest of the ingredients and pour in enough water to cover.

7. Bring to mixture to a simmer on medium low, skimming fat off the surface as the broth cooks.

8. Reduce heat to low and cook for another 5 hours, continuing to skim surface.

9. Strain through a fine mesh sieve to remove large particles into a resealable container.

7. White Stock

This stock is perfect for white sauces and gravies and tastes delicious with turkey or lamb. I like to make it for holidays when I have the family over.

Preparation Time-15 minutes

Servings-16

Ingredients

- 1 veal knuckle, meat cut from the bone
- 48 ounces chicken
- 2 celery stalks
- 1 turnip
- 1 yellow onion
- 1 carrots
- 1/3 ounce salt
- 128 ounces water

Directions

1. Combine all ingredients in a large stock pot and bring mixture to a boil.

2. Reduce heat and cover the pot. Simmer for 5-6 hours.

3. Strain mixture through a fine mesh strainer into another pot and discard solids.

4. Save chicken and veal for other recipes.

8.Quick chicken stock

This is the perfect stock recipe when you have some leftover chicken bones. I freeze this and use it for soups and gravies for months.

Preparation Time-15 minutes

Servings-16

Ingredients

- 1 large onion, cut in 4 wedges
- 1 quartered large carrot
- 1 quartered stalk celery
- 1 rotisserie chicken carcass
- 15 whole black peppercorns
- 10 cloves garlic
- 128 ounces cold water
- 1 teaspoon sea salt

Directions

1. Combine carrot, onion, celery, chicken, peppercorns and garlic in a large pressure cooker. Pour water into the pot until 2/3 of the way full and seal the lid

2. Bring cooker to full pressure on high. Reduce the heat to the medium and cook for 30 minutes.

3. Remove pressure cooker from heat and let pressure drop slowly. Remove lid and pour stock into a strainer to remove solids and cool to room temperature. Skim fat off the surface of the stock and store in the refrigerator.

9.Roasted Chicken Broth

I like to serve roasted chicken at special family events but I don't like all the waste. This broth is simple to prepare and stores very well.

Preparation Time-25 minutes

Servings-4

Ingredients

- 54 ounces chicken, giblets removed
- 1 peeled onion, cut in quarters
- 1 chopped rib celery
- 1/3 ounces kosher salt
- 3 lightly smashed cloves garlic
- ½ ounce ketchup
- 32 ounces cold water,

Directions

1. Preheat the oven to 400 degrees Fahrenheit

2. Combine chicken, chopped celery and onion in a large Dutch oven. Season with salt.

3. Bake in oven for 1 hour until chicken is no longer pink in the center and reads 160 degrees Fahrenheit with a meat thermometer

4. Place roasted chicken on a plate and cool. Remove meat from chicken bone and set aside.

5. Remove fat from Dutch Oven and place on stove on medium high heat. Place chicken bones and meat from thighs and drumsticks in the pot.

6. Stir in the rest of the ingredients and bring to a boil. Scrape the bottom of the Dutch oven to dislodge food particles.

7. Remove the chicken fat from the Dutch oven, leaving the brown flavor bits on the bottom of your Dutch oven.

8. Reduce heat and simmer for 3-4 hours. Add more water if needed.

9. Skim fat off the surface as you simmer. Strain and discard solids.

10.Smoked turkey broth

This broth is perfect for all those turkey bones you collect at Thanksgiving. I store it in the freezer and use it for gravy for my leftovers.

Preparation Time-25 minutes

Servings-24

Ingredients

- 2 smoked turkey legs
- 1 large halved red onion
- 1 large halved Spanish onion
- 1 large carrot, chopped into three chunks
- 1 large seeded red pepper
- ½ ounce olive oil
- 224 ounces cold water
- 5 lightly smashed cloves garlic
- 10 whole black peppercorns
- salt
- 8 ounces water

Directions

1. Preheat oven to 400 degrees Fahrenheit.

2. Place turkey, onions, carrot and pepper in a roasting pan and brush with olive oil.

3. Roast for 15 minutes until browned

4. Pour water into a large stockpot on medium. Transfer turkey mixture to the stockpot and bring to a boil. Reduce heat and simmer.

5. Place roasting pan on the stove burner and heat drippings in the pan until sizzling.

6. Add 8 ounces of water to the roasting pan and scrape food particles on the bottom to dislodge.

7. Pour roasting pan mixture into the stockpot

8. Continue to simmer for 6-8 hours and skim fat off the surface occasionally.

9. Strain and discard solids. Store broth in a sealable container in the refrigerator.

11.Instant Pot Oxtail Broth

This oxtail broth is tasty and satisfying when used in gravy and sauces. The Instant Pot cooks the broth to perfection in half the time.

Preparation Time-5 minutes

Servings-8

Ingredients

- 32 ounces oxtail
- 1 bunch chopped green onions
- 3 smashed garlic cloves
- ¼ ounce ground ginger
- 56 ounces water

Directions

1. Place rack 6" from heat in the oven and preheat broiler.

2. Line a baking sheet with foil and arrange oxtail on the sheet. Broil for 5-7 minutes each side until browned.

3. Put oxtail in an Instant Pot and top with onions, garlic and ginger. Pour in enough water to cover.

4. Close lid on the Instant Pot and select pressure according to manufacturer's instructions. Cook for 60 minutes.

5. Slowly release pressure according to instructions, then remove lid.

6. Let mixture cool and strain. Discard solids and store in the refrigerator.

12.Shrimp Stock

This shrimp stock makes a delicious fish sauce for your next seafood meal. I use the shells from fresh jumbo shrimp.

Preparation Time-20 minutes

Servings-4

Ingredients

- shrimp shells from 32 ounces of shrimp
- 4 ounces onion, roughly chopped
- 1 sliced lemon
- 2 ounces celery, roughly chopped
- 2 ounces celery leaves
- 2 crushed garlic cloves
- 1 teaspoon whole black peppercorns
- 3 sprigs fresh thyme
- 2 bay leaves
- 64 ounces cold water

Directions

1. Combine all ingredients in a large pan and bring to a boil.

2. Reduce heat to low and cook for 1 hour until liquid is reduced by half. Skim foam off the surface as you cook.

3. Strain broth and store in the freezer until ready to use.

13.Fast Chicken Soup Base

Chicken soup is the perfect cure for a bad cold or flu. I keep this stock handy for those times when I need a health boost.

Preparation Time-20 minutes

Servings-8

Ingredients

- 64 ounces chicken broth

- 32 ounces water

- 1 rotisserie chicken carcass

- 1 ½ ounces vegetable oil

- 2 large diced onions

- 2 large peeled carrots, cut into medallions

- 1 teaspoon dried thyme leaves

- 2 large stalks celery, cut into ¼" thick pieces

Directions

1. Pour chicken broth and water in a large soup kettle and bring to a simmer on medium high heat.

2. Remove chicken from bones and remove skin. Set meat aside and place bones and skin in the soup kettle.

3. Reduce heat and cover the kettle partially. Simmer for 20-30 minutes.

4. Strain broth and discard solids.

5. Sauté oil, onions, celery and carrots in the kettle for 8-10 minutes until tender.

6. Stir in broth, chicken and thyme and bring mixture to a simmer.

7. Use immediately or store in the refrigerator before use.

14.Chicken Broth in Slow cooker

I like using the slow cooker for broths because I can set it and leave it overnight. The flavours in this broth blend together in a perfect symphony of taste.

Preparation Time-20 minutes

Servings-5

Ingredients

- 40 ounces chicken pieces, bone-in
- 48 ounces water
- 2 chopped stalks celery
- 2 chopped carrots
- 1 quartered onion
- ½ ounce dried basil

Directions

1. Place all ingredients in a slow cooker and cook on Low for 8-10 hours. Strain broth and discard solids. Remove meat from the chicken bones and use in soup or for another purpose.

15.Basic Vegetable Stock

This stock makes a delicious base for vegetable sauce or soup. Store this vegetable stock in the freezer for a quick soup base with celery and carrots.

Preparation Time-20 minutes

Servings-12

Ingredients

- ½ ounce olive oil
- 1 large chopped onion, chopped in 1" chunks
- 2 chopped stalks celery, chopped in 1" chunks
- 2 large chopped carrots, chopped in 1" chunks
- 1 bunch chopped green onions, chopped in 1" chunks
- 8 minced cloves garlic
- 6 sprigs fresh thyme
- 8 sprigs fresh parsley
- 1 teaspoon salt
- 2 bay leaves
- 64 ounces water

Directions

1. Heat olive oil in large stockpot and sauté onion, carrots, celery, garlic, scallions, parsley, bay leaves and thyme in the oil for 5-10 minutes on high. Stir often.

2. Season with salt and pour in water. Bring mixture to a boil.

3. Reduce heat to medium low and simmer for 35 minutes.

4. Strain broth and discard solids.

16.Best Vegetable Broth

Here is another delicious recipe for vegetable broth that works well in a hearty soup. When you have leftover vegetables in the fridge, throw them into this broth.

Preparation Time-20 minutes

Servings-8

Ingredients

- 16 ounces chopped celery, leaves removed
- 24 ounces sweet onions
- 16 ounces carrots, sliced into 1" pieces
- 16 ounces cored tomatoes
- 16 ounces green bell pepper, sliced into 1" pieces
- 8 ounces cubed turnips
- 1 ounce extra-virgin olive oil
- 3 whole cloves
- 3 cloves garlic
- 1 bay leaf
- 1 chopped bunch fresh parsley
- 6 whole black peppercorns
- 128 ounces water

Directions

1. Preheat oven to 450 degrees Fahrenheit

2. In a large bowl, toss carrots, onions, tomatoes, turnips and peppers in olive oil until coated.

3. Move the vegetables to a roasting pan and cook for 60-75 minutes, stirring every 15-20 minutes. Cook until vegetables have browned and onions are caramelized.

4. Transfer roasted vegetables, celery, bay leaf, garlic, parsley, peppercorn and water in a large pot. Bring the mixture to a boil, reduce heat to medium low and simmer for 35-45 minutes until liquid is reduced by half.

5. Strain broth and set solids aside for use in soup or other uses.

17.Delicious Chicken stock

I love the flavour of ginger in this recipe. This healthy stock is perfect for warming the belly on a cold day.

Preparation Time-20 minutes

Servings-14

Ingredients

- 64 ounces chicken
- 56 ounces water
- 1 large halved onion
- 3 stalks celery
- 1 teaspoon fresh ginger, grated
- 3 carrots, sliced into 2" pieces
- 1 bay leaf
- salt

Directions

1. Put chicken in a large stockpot on High. Add enough water to cover chicken and bring mixture to a boil.

2. Reduce heat and simmer for 60 minutes on medium-low

3. Take chicken out of the pot, reserving all liquid in the stockpot.

4. All chicken to cool and remove meat and skin from bones.

5. Add skin and bones to the stockpot and store meat for use later. Add the rest of the ingredients to the stockpot and simmer for 3-4 hours.

6. Strain broth and discard any solids. Store in the refrigerator.

18.Basic Beef Stock

You can get basic soup bones at the butchers that are specially kept for this stock. Use the extra celery you have leftover from the stalk as part of this soup.

Preparation Time-20 minutes

Servings-8

Ingredients

- 124 ounces beef soup bones
- 3 large chopped carrots, cut in 1" chunks
- 1 large quartered onion, root end trimmed
- 4 ounces water
- 2 chopped stalks celery, cut in thirds
- 1 large chopped tomato
- 4 ounces parsnip, chopped
- 1 medium potato, chopped into chunks
- 8 whole black peppercorns
- 4 sprigs chopped fresh parsley
- 1 bay leaf
- ½ ounce salt
- 1/3 ounce dried thyme
- 2 cloves garlic
- 96 ounces water

Directions

1. Preheat oven to 450 degrees Fahrenheit

2. Place bones, carrots and onion in a larger roasting pan and bake for 35 minutes until bones are browned. Turn mixture frequently.

3. Drain fat from the roasting and transfer mixture to a large stockpot.

4. Pour 4 ounces of water into the roasting pan and scrape the bottom to dislodge food particles with a wooden spoon. Pour liquid into the stockpot.

5. Add the rest of the ingredients into the stockpot and bring mixture to a boil. Reduce heat to medium low, cover and simmer broth for 5-6 hours.

6. Strain stock and discard solids. Store in the freezer until ready to use.

19.Roasted Vegetable stock

The flavour of roasted vegetables is amazing in this stock and making it is really easy. I like to use this for creamy sauce to pour on steamed veggies and mashed potatoes.

Preparation Time-35 minutes

Servings-8

Ingredients

- 1 whole head garlic, head cut off
- 4 chopped carrots
- 4 chopped stalks celery
- 3 chopped onions
- 1 green bell pepper, cut in quarters
- 1 quartered tomato
- 2 ½ ounces olive oil
- salt and pepper
- 64 ounces water
- ¼ ounce dried thyme
- ¼ ounce dried parsley
- 2 bay leaves

Directions

1. Preheat oven to 400 degrees Fahrenheit.

2. On a baking sheet lined with foil, arrange carrots, garlic head, celery, bell pepper, onions and tomato. Drizzle the vegetables with the oil and then sprinkle with the salt and pepper.

3. Place vegetables in the oven for 60-70 minutes until brown and softened. Turn vegetables every 25 minutes as you roast them.

4. Mix water, parsley, thyme and bay leaves in a large pot and heat on medium high.

5. Squeeze the garlic from the head into the pot and discard outer peel.

6. Place all roasted vegetables in the pot and bring mixture to a boil.

7. Reduce the heat to medium low and simmer for 75 minutes. Strain broth and store in the refrigerator.

20.Seafood gumbo stock

When you want to make gumbo that tastes fresh and delicious, this is the stock for you. I like to serve this with some rice and steamed vegetables.

Preparation Time-15 minutes

Servings-8

Ingredients

- shells from 16 ounces shrimp
- 4 sliced carrots
- 4 onions, cut in quarters
- ½ bunch sliced celery
- 2 bay leaves
- 3 sliced garlic cloves
- 5 whole cloves
- 2 sprigs fresh parsley
- ½ ounce dried basil
- 1 teaspoon ground black pepper
- 160 ounces water
- 1/3 ounce dried thyme

Directions

1. Preheat oven to 375 degrees Fahrenheit. Line a baking sheet with foil and arrange shrimp shells on the sheet.

2. Bake shells for 10 minutes until edges brown

3. Mix all ingredients in a large stockpot and bring mixture to a boil.

4. Reduce heat and cook for 5-7 hours. Pour in more water as needed.

5. Strain stock and discard solids. Pour liquid back into the pot and heat until liquid is reduced to 64 ounces of broth.

21.Vegetable stock

Make this stock with some fresh butternut squash and kosher salt. I prefer the creamy flavour of this stock when I make sauces.

Preparation Time-15 minutes

Servings-6

Ingredients

- ½ ounce extra-virgin olive oil
- 2 chopped onions
- 1 chopped celery root
- 8 ounces potato peelings
- 8 ounces carrots, chopped
- 8 ounces fresh mushrooms
- 8 ounces butternut squash, peel and pulp
- salt
- 32 ounces water

Directions

1. Heat olive oil in a stockpot on medium low heat and sauté onions in the oil for 20 minutes until golden brown and softened.

2. Add celery, potato, carrots, squash and mushrooms in the stockpot and mix well. Season with salt and cook for 45 minutes until vegetables are browned and softened.

3. Add water to stockpot and bring mixture to a boil. Reduce heat and simmer broth for 40 minutes. Stir often.

4. Strain broth and discard solids. Store in the freezer until ready to use.

22. Dashi Stock

This dashi stock is added to soy sauce or mirin and poured over rice for a tasty garnish. This stock is simple to make and adds a delicious flavour to most fish recipes.

Preparation Time-15 minutes

Servings-8

Ingredients

- 1 ounce dried kelp, gently wiped of dirt
- 32 ounces water
- 4 ounces bonito flakes

Directions

1. Combine kelp and water in a large pan and soak for 35 minutes until tender

2. Remove kelp and slice several slits into the leaf along the length

3. Place kelp back in the water and bring to a boil.

4. Remove kelp as soon as the water boils.

5. Add flakes to the water in the pan and bring liquid back to a boil. Remove pan from heat and cool. The bonito flakes will settle at the bottom of the pan.

6. Strain liquid through a cheesecloth and store in the freezer until ready to use.

23. Bone Broth with Turmeric and Ginger

Turmeric is a healthy spice that reduces inflammation. If you suffer from any auto-immune diseases, this broth will help with the symptoms.

Preparation Time-15 minutes

Servings-6

Ingredients

- 1 rotisserie chicken carcass
- 2 chopped carrots
- 8 ounces celery, chopped
- ½ ounce apple cider vinegar
- 1/3 ounce ground turmeric
- 3 cloves garlic
- 1 teaspoon fresh ginger root, minced
- 32 ounces warm water

Directions

1. Combine all ingredients in an Instant Pot. Lock the lid and select function according to manufacturer's instructions. Cook for 1 ½ hours.

2. Slowly release pressure on the Instant pot. Unlock lid and strain the broth through a fine mesh strainer. Discard solids and store broth in the freezer until ready to use.

24.Grandma's Chicken Stock

My grandmother used this stock as a base for her famous chicken soup. Throw in some matzoh balls, egg noodles and dumplings to make this soup a real meal.

Preparation Time-15 minutes

Servings-8

Ingredients

- 128 ounces chicken
- 3 chopped stalks celery
- 1 onion, cut in quarter

Directions

1. Place all ingredients in a large pot and cover with water. Bring mixture to a boil.

2. Skim fat off surface as you boil. Reduce heat and simmer for 2-3 hours.

3. Pour broth through a strainer and remove solids.

25.Beef Shank Broth

I like to use this broth to make a dark, rich gravy that adds flavour to roast beef and mashed potatoes. I have also used it for beef stew with hearty vegetables.

Preparation Time-25 minutes

Servings-8

Ingredients

- 96 ounces water
- 16 ounces beef shank
- 4 ounces pearled barley
- 1 coarsely chopped carrot
- ½ peeled turnip, chopped
- 1 sliced leek
- 2 chopped stalks celery
- ½ ounce dried thyme
- 4 ounces fresh parsley, chopped
- salt and pepper

Directions

1. Boil water in a large stockpot.

2. Add beef, carrot, barley, leek, turnip and celery in the water. Season with salt, pepper and thyme and bring back up to a boil.

3. Reduce heat and simmer for 2 hours. Remove beef shank and cut meat into small pieces.

4. Place meat back in the stockpot and discard bone.

5. Return mixture back to a boil and add parsley. Stir in well.

26.Pressure Cooker Beef Stock

I use an Instant Pot to make this stock because it is easy and takes less time than a crockpot. I like to mix this beef stock in my chunky beef stew with carrots, celery and potatoes.

Preparation Time-15 minutes

Servings-14

Ingredients

- 16 ounces beef bones
- 1 large unpeeled sweet onion, halved
- 4 large carrots, chopped into 4" pieces
- 4 ribs celery, chopped into 4" pieces
- 4 cloves garlic, cut in half
- 1 bunch flat-leaf parsley
- ½ ounce salt
- 1 teaspoon dried thyme
- 1 teaspoon whole black peppercorns
- 2 bay leaves
- 128 ounces water

Directions

1. Preheat oven to 425 degrees Fahrenheit

2. Line baking sheet with foil and arrange beef bones on the sheet. Bake for 15-20 minutes.

3. Place onions on the baking sheet and bake for another 45 minutes.

4. Transfer onion and bones to a pressure cooker. Add the rest of the ingredients and lock lid.

5. Cook for 1 hour. Release pressure slowly from the cooker and strain broth.

27.Vegan Dashi Soup stock

This vegan stock is perfect for those who have cut meat and eggs out of their diets. I use fresh kombu that I find at a local grocery store.

Preparation Time-5 minutes

Servings-4

Ingredients

- 13 ½ ounces water
- 2" square of kelp
- 1 ¼ ounces soy sauce
- 1 ounce mirin
- ½ ounce sake

Directions

Bring water and konbu to a simmer in a large pan. Add the rest of the ingredients and continue to simmer for 5 minutes. Stir occasionally.

Strain stock and remove konbu. Cool stock and store in the refrigerator until ready to use.

28.Pork Chop Tokotsu Broth

This pork chop broth tastes amazing when mixed with some hearty vegetables and pork meat. I use fresh pork chops from the butcher for the freshest taste.

Preparation Time-15 minutes

Servings-2

Ingredients

- 1 pork chop, bone-in, meat and fat cut from bone
- 32 ounces water
- ¼ onion, chopped
- 1/3 ounce chicken base
- 1 clove garlic

Directions

1. Cut pork chop meat into small pieces.

2. Combine meat bone, fat and pork chop meat in a large pan. Add the rest of the ingredients and bring mixture to a boil.

3. Reduce heat to medium low, cover the pan and simmer for 5-6 hours. Add more water if needed.

4. Strain mixture and separate bones. Place the meat and half of the liquid in a food processor. Blend well and return to the pan.

5. Strain broth and store in the refrigerator.

29. Egyptian Chicken Broth

This broth has a delicious international flavour with cardamom and cloves. Use this to make sauce for vegetables and rice.

Preparation Time-15 minutes

Servings-4

Ingredients

- 1 whole chicken with giblets, cut in quarters
- salt
- ground black pepper
- 1 ounce clarified butter
- 1 trimmed onion
- 4 whole cloves
- 4 cardamom pods
- 1 bay leaf
- 32 ounces water

Directions

1. Season chicken with salt and pepper and rub the seasonings into the meat.

2. Mix chicken, chicken giblets and clarified butter in a large stock pot. Heat on Medium and add the rest of the ingredients except for water. Stir often until liquid is evaporated.

3. Cook for 3-5 minutes until chicken is browned lightly.

4. Pour in enough water to cover chicken and simmer for 25 minutes. Strain and store in the refrigerator.

30.Scotch Broth

This lamb broth has a delicious mild flavour that tastes amazing when used in soup and stew. Try slicing up extra vegetables and pouring this stock as a gravy.

Preparation Time-30 minutes

Servings-8

Ingredients

- 36 ounce leg of lamb
- 64 ounces water
- 3 chopped onions
- 3 chopped turnips
- 2 chopped carrots
- ½ ounce whole black peppercorns
- 4 ounces barley
- 1 diced carrot
- 2 minced onions
- 1 chopped leek
- 1 diced stalk celery
- 2 diced turnips

Directions

1. Combine lamb, water, 3 onions, 2 carrots, 3 turnips and peppercorns in a large stockpot and bring to a boil.

2. Reduce heat to a simmer, cover the pot and cook for 3-4 hours. Skim fat from the surface as you cook.

3. Strain liquid and remove meat and bones. Chop meat into small pieces and store into the refrigerator. Discard vegetables.

4. Add barley to a large bowl and pour in enough water to cover. Soak barley for 1 hour.

5. Reheat stock in a pot and add barley, diced carrot, minced onions, chopped leek, diced celery and diced turnips.

6. Bring mixture to a boil. Reduce heat and simmer for 35 minutes until vegetables are tender.

7. Return meat back to the pot and simmer for another 5 minutes.

Conclusion

From beef to chicken, vegetable to shrimp, the combinations of stocks and broths recipes are endless. Buying a mix at the store is easy, but does it taste as fresh as homemade? What do you do with that leftover lamb bone or beef shank once you finish dinner and the dishes are clean? The flavour left over in the bones can make a healthy and hearty soup or gravy and takes little skill to make. When a homemade broth is what you are after, give one of these recipes a try.

About the Author

A native of Albuquerque, New Mexico, Sophia Freeman found her calling in the culinary arts when she enrolled at the Sante Fe School of Cooking. Freeman decided to take a year after graduation and travel around Europe, sampling the cuisine from small bistros and family owned restaurants from Italy to Portugal. Her bubbly personality and inquisitive nature made her popular with the locals in the villages and when she finished her trip and came home, she had made friends for life in the places she had visited. She also came home with a deeper understanding of European cuisine.

Freeman went to work at one of Albuquerque's 5-star restaurants as a sous-chef and soon worked her way up to head chef. The restaurant began to feature Freeman's original dishes as specials on the menu and soon after, she began to write e-books with her recipes. Sophia's dishes mix local flavours with European inspiration making them irresistible to the diners in her restaurant and the online community.

Freeman's experience in Europe didn't just teach her new ways of cooking, but also unique methods of presentation. Using rich sauces, crisp vegetables and meat cooked to perfection, she creates a stunning display as well as a delectable dish. She has won many local awards for her cuisine and she continues to delight her diners with her culinary masterpieces.

Author's Afterthoughts

I want to convey my big thanks to all of my readers who have taken the time to read my book. Readers like you make my work so rewarding and I cherish each and every one of you.

Grateful cannot describe how I feel when I know that someone has chosen my work over all of the choices available online. I hope you enjoyed the book as much as I enjoyed writing it.

Feedback from my readers is how I grow and learn as a chef and an author. Please take the time to let me know your thoughts by leaving a review on Amazon so I and your fellow readers can learn from your experience.

My deepest thanks,

Sophia Freeman

Printed in Dunstable, United Kingdom

68324717R10051